STFU: THOUGHTS & FEELINGS

By Ellevan

Index

Prologue

To say there's a simple trick to "*being mindful*" would be misleading. It's a practice. To try and create a sudden change, that just l*ooks like a miracle*, is unhelpful. ***The shift you want takes work.*** The most worthy work one can find.

To take responsibility for our *state of being* and what you attract may just be the very activity *we as sentient beings* are here to uncover at this time in evolution.

If you're familiar with the concept of the *Tao,* you'd know that *trying*, at all, is counterproductive.

We'll get into *the art of allowing* later, but I wanted to start off by saying that *separation* is a huge *misconception*.

In the quantum field, there is no "separation of matter" between you and I, or anything. It's all part of the *same energy field* and, ultimately, the same consciousness; having an experience through different view points.

Humans often live in jails they create in their *own head.* Whether they think it serves some body or some purpose to experience pain and discomfort, or they're just not aware of their thoughts and feelings so they keep manifesting painful experiences, it's silly.

It'd be a shame if a human had an entire lifetime with out *at least realizing* their mistakes and making an *earnest attempt* at bettering themselves and their experiences.

There's a deep knowing that this, i*ntelligent observation of things*, belongs to a *higher source*, and we're an extended player in the game.

So, how to access this power? How to be sure it's flowing ***with*** *you?*

Chapter 1: Uncovering the Pain Addiction

Most of us have built little systems in our thought patterns. Like we've been led to believe that pain is valuable. That it serves a driving force or has some form of pay off. "Work Hard" - "Big boys don't cry" - "Hustle".

What about: release pressure from the thought you'd like to manifest and allow it to flow into your experience?

Seems a lot easier...

Taking your foot off the gas in this repetitive system you've built for yourself is quite possibly the most *difficult* part of the mindful journey.

In the beginning, you must *retrain your mind from **"fighting the disease"** to **"creating the cure"***.

Instead of focusing on the problem and bringing more of that into your experience, you focus on the solution and manifest.

There's a couple helpful ways to get out of your old patterns and they all include *shutting the fuck up.*

Be prepared to mentally do this, or stop reading here.

Now that we're past the victim mentality, we can start realizing that there is no outside world. There's just how we remember it and how we feel about it. *Every person you've ever met, every thing you've ever seen, and anything you've ever done—all in your head.*

Okay, let's do an exercise. Take the most recent painful situation you were in. Someone yelled at you, you were wronged, or things didn't go your way. Imagine yourself in that situation, right before it happened...

Knowing how you proceeded and reacted, erase that memory from your identity right now. In that moment, before things went south, *take a deep breath*, smile at the person and say: "I am so happy we could share this moment! But, I have to go."

They greet you and you walk out, heading to another place that appreciates you for who you are. You had a great time.

Phew! Dodged a bullet there. Congrats!

Doesn't that feel nicer? Even if it's not *really what happened. Doesn't it serve your being by having a lighter heart?* Instead of re-stabbing yourself with the knife that hits you every time you think about it? *Why pay rent for somewhere you don't even live?*

If every *tough situation* is a teacher, you learn the lesson and move on. Like with every human teacher, you don't need to keep taking the course, unless you ***still have something to learn from it.***

This is often the key to letting things go. *Find the key in it.* Realize if *you're still hurt*. Your higher being has all the healing for you right on the other side of the *responsibility* you take for it. Reasons you may not be in alignment about it? Your human self wants to be "right" or "forgiven", whether you can currently identify this or not.

Explore the pain as an observer, *in order to release it.*

Whatever way you slice it, we all participate. We just hate that we didn't have the tools to avoid the situation or feel the shame of being there in the first place.

Shame helps nobody, especially you. *So allow yourself* to get over the pain addiction. Leave the past in the past. ***It's over.*** You can choose this amazing life ahead, or *choose* to *focus on the past* and remain out of alignment with the now. Seems like a simple choice.

Chapter 2: Catching Inspiration

Once you take responsibility for how you feel, you're so free. You're freer than free. You can go, do, create and be anything! No more chains on your heart!

And YOU made the choice.

Now, in your new realm where nobody owes you anything, you can proceed with your whole heart. It's time to catch inspiration! The key to *the next logical step.*

I have found that forcing *anything*, never works. So we must take action only when truly inspired. Not because our idol did things this way, or you heard this type of thing worked for so and so. Listen to who you are and think about how things could play out, *in the best way possible.*

Dream forward, *then let it all go.* Dream up a *fun dream*, then proceed with your present day. Live life as scheduled but *allow the feelings* of a pre-manifested future (*idea*) to inspire the feeling state of now. *Now. And NOW!*

Inspiration comes in many forms. You really have to be open to *symbols of communication* from the universe.

I'll listen for words *I hear* when people walk by, first glances on a page, or even just observe my surroundings. As tools *guiding my direction* as where to place my focus. For instance, the universe trained me to look for *11:11* as an affirmation that I was on the right track. That my current *objective is in-line* with what my purpose is.

Sometimes this doesn't seem centered around self, either! Sometimes it's to low-key help someone else.

Follow it and end up learning something that helps with your main narrative later.

Essentially, be open to ***giving***. Then you're open for ***receiving***.

—

One time, when the universe was communicating that I was on track with my feeling state, at a big influencer festival in Washington D.C. heading back to my hotel at 3 am after remotely recording a podcast, "I'd love to grab a pizza," I say, but immediately *let it go.*

Just felt good about the *idea of a pizza*.

When I saw the lobby bar was closed, I chuckled and moved on. It *was* 3:00 am. Back at my lobby, usually filled with screaming teenagers, was a ghost town. Other than a new friend standing solo, holding 2 boxes of pizza...

"Dude!" He says, as I danced towards him, "I just ordered a pizza before I hit the sack and the delivery guy accidentally gave me two! No way I can eat this all. Want one?"

My mind was ***blown****.*

Something as simple as a *pizza* could appear in place of the universe, *showing me that I was in alignment.*

Flowing effortlessly, I was manifesting at a rapid pace!

Desires are just fuel to focus on our creations.

It doesn't matter how it gets there. It will come through if you're in harmony.

If we can *appreciate* but not *desperately need.*

The universe *loves* this language. It's gentle. It feels easy. Pizza can flow into our life on this easy vibration.

Manifest that easy pizza friends. Whatever your toppings.

(P.S. - I brought that *fresh, hot deluxe* up to my room full of drunk creators, and they went nuts!)

Good feelings expand when you share the blessings!

This brings us to our next concept: there is *no lack. It's almost like that was made up to keep you in fear...*

Chapter 3: Abundance

There can not be this much stuff already if there was a limit on stuff. Anything you can dream of can be ***created***.

Everything you've ever wanted is waiting for you.

Plus, no one can access your stuff. We all have our *own stuff.* A vortex of creation. Everything you wish for is in there. *Often, just ideas that represent "success" to you, anyway. I digress.*

Want a nice car? Why? It'll feel awesome. That's okay. Don't wrong yourself for wanting things. If it has manifested, it *needs* appreciators of it. There's no virtue to petty small living. You're not helping anyone else by giving less to yourself. In fact, *living in a state of lack only creates more of it in the universe.* ***Never think you're doing anyone else a favour by not embracing your full abundance.*** You have it. Allow it in. Move on.

All we have to realize is, *the amount of **abundance** you've been letting in is equivalent to the amount of **self worth** you have.*

Ever wonder how some financially abundant people are sometimes...dense? "Easy on the thinking"?

It's because having prosperity isn't about how *intellectually smart* you are. It's about how much you believe you should have it.

In fact, sometimes being a little simple can work in their favour! They don't waste time speculating, they just go for it. [DJ _____!!] While a whiz is on their high moral ground, trying to calculate and control the dense ones simply approach with abundant faith and actually manifest their dream!

By feeling their way into it.

Feelings must be the most misunderstood tool of this time. If there weren't already 100 ad's that reached you today *(assuming you read in the morning)*, you may realize that your feelings are up to you, and only you.

There's business in *sad*. But, there's not a purchase in the world that could heal you like a conversation *with self* could. But that understanding is *free* and doesn't sell fixes. It won't turn consumers into ambassadors like marketable band aid's do. In fact, it turns those who learn this into fully capable people all by themselves. This is NOT good for business.

Now you say: "WTF? Didn't this dude just say prosperity is good? *So, selling must be good.*"

And I'd say: "Yes! Selling and making money IS good! But be aware of when you're being marketed to, who's benefiting from it, and why."

This is a fun helpful practice for daily human self awareness. Go to a business. You know what you're getting, it's fair. You're an adult who makes their own decisions.

But consider if you are sold on an ad campaign. Especially ones that sell improvements *without doing any work*. Get addicted to doing the *thought work*, or at very least become aware of these transactions and expectations.

Abundance is everywhere around us.

Look at a tree. Did it hesitate to grow that hundredth branch? *Not at all.* Did the air not breeze in one direction because it was *saving* it for another direction, another time? *No, it just blew.* ***Whatever is needed, will always be provided.*** The force of life just has to be backed by *absolute faith*.

This brings us to our next issue: belief.

Chapter 4: Belief

I had a broken heart from my own thoughts.

I was running a program, mentally, that held my identity captive. My evolution was on hold until I found the values in my lessons, applied them to my circumstance, and made adjustments that I needed to flow in the right direction.

"You don't need to know the exact goal to start moving towards it. So, move."—So, I did.

I began to see these *plays* in life. Segments.

If I took my time, so would they. I was finally *present*, and ready to really believe.

Meeting me anytime before that you'd think, "he's a confident guy! I'm sure he feels great about himself." Wrong. *I felt horrible.* I was constantly winning over people so I could feel appreciated and loved because I didn't do that for myself.

I wasn't sure if something happened, and only I was there to appreciate it; that it was *worth* the same, if someone else saw it. *Essentially, I forgot that I am the God of my experiences.*

—

I watched my pops serve people.

Literally, he was a waiter, and a great one!

I remember sitting at this little ocean side Italian restaurant, in the 90's. Seeing my father work his charm on a table of full breed Italians. In 5 minutes, they went from strangers to best friends, and I couldn't imagine what words he used to get such emotion out of people he just met.

I was fascinated, with causing a *feeling* reaction. I felt a calling to create moments right then and there.

Something I later built a career off of, in my own way. But

there certainly wasn't a lack of years that I *just sucked* at life...

I figured if I could get *someone else* to believe in me, I could one day believe in me. Years of shouting my entire resume at people during networking opportunities, painstaking attempts at landing gigs with *clever jargon* instead of just doing the work and *really stupid* campaigns that led no where...

All because I was trying to get validation before I had the goods to give. I needed attention. *I got it, too!*

One of the dearest things about humans is: we're all kind of lost. So, we entertain somebody else's ideas before we listen to ourselves sometimes.

As a producer, and a *budding thought leader* (haha), I remind people that they don't actually need me, or anyone!

Sing your song. Live your life. Fuck everyone else.

But that's not why we do it. We don't always do it for ourselves. We do it to prove to others that we're worthy. *I was masterful at this.*

Sporting a process similar to a shark in the sea, I'd secretly watch the person of interest, observe what they felt connected to, mentally collect every thing associated with those ideas, place myself in front of them, and ***BOOM!*** *Spew the script of their dreams! Coasting on excited reactions, I made new friends daily and started a business once a month.*

As exciting as it all felt, it lead to nothing. I was empty still. The drive would die. My energy would zone out and I'd focus on the next hit. The next validation. *I was dating.*

What changes the need for exterior validation?

Taking responsibility.

I thought that someone was going to give me my dreams.

I thought that one day, someone might have the answer for me. That I'd be taken somewhere by someone unlikely to a better place. ***How stupid.***

Nobody knows what YOU want. You have to build it. And find a way to be happy with the early stages. There's no other way. And this requires BELIEF.

If you don't full heartedly believe that you, and only you, are here to do the thing, in the specific way that you do that thing, then don't even start. *Keep flailing.* You'll eventually find it. But, the thing you go home and do. The thing you buy magazine's about. You're here to do ***that*** thing. Don't worry about what someone told you. Follow the bliss of how it makes you feel. Be alone with it. Let it comfort you. Choose to believe in yourself because of it. *It's worth it.*

You proceeding with your purpose and failing is a million times better than faking it for others and "winning" on their terms. You can only *truly believe* in ***that*** thing. Your higher being won't go to the other places.

If you wish to unleash the flow of abundance, that's waiting for you, find your true knowing.

As you move towards the craft, lifestyle or vocation you want, you'll start to naturally uncover why you haven't taken the time to fully believe yet.

Often, it's because we've been disappointed and learned to *fear that pain.* So, you keep your next idea on the "back burner" until further notice. But, fuck that. Fail on your own time, yes. But KEEP failing. Don't let fear guide your ship. Your home is what you make it. This is all temporary anyway. Might as well commit to something you care about.

Believe in yourself. It is easier.

Chapter 5: Navigating The "Outside World"

Gaining this awareness and co-existing with others is not an overnight progression. You're always in practice, attempting to be mindful. At first, you're probably pretty trash at it. *Hopping into the ring thinking you're a gold medalist right away and getting knocked out by the rough winds of life.*

The work is never done, so don't think by reading my very informative and hilariously helpful book, that you got it all figured. *Life will keep giving you* ***new problems*** *for you to create* ***new solutions*** *for.*

Even in my chosen career, with influential friends and all the affirmations someone could ask for, I still had confusion about whether or not I could "make it".

"I'm having an issue with wavering faith" I said.

My wise bearded friend led me to see that *we only start to trip from our own expectation not being fulfilled.* ***And only we can control that.***

If we set the bar a little lower, just to work with ourselves from where we currently are, things get a little easier.

It's not rocket science to think I'm not gonna have *10 foot anxiety* jumping a *5 foot pole*, but sometimes you just need to hear it. So, I *started letting go* of what I thought I "deserved" or where I thought I "should be at" based on talent or hustle. Started living from where I was at. Enjoying the experiences I've had and what I *was* recognized for.

It wasn't where I would be forever, but I realized it *was* past where I thought I could be when I started out!

I always dreamt of "stardom", but never actually seen it through in my mind.

I knew I was great. But, couldn't envision my win, at first.

The "outside world", meaning the already manifested 3rd dimension. Physical matter—humans, the post office, the cat down the street, ya know, "out there".

These people want answers. They expect you to be a part of that thing they have turning out there. And, to be honest, you kind of should. They're fulfilling their part as best they can and it is up to you to decide what part you want to play, if any. When they grill us about our endeavours, they're not attacking, they're probably intrigued! Just not as sensitive, and that may not feel nice. Consider, if you're sharing too early as well. Let ideas grow in your head before you spread the energy of it around. ***This helps with manifesting.***

Nobody attaches the same preciousness to your dream that you do. So, don't let it effect you when they imply that you won't make it. Honestly, in *their* classic sense of "making it" you probably won't! But, that's not your journey to fulfill. *That's something they saw on television and want to be closer to.* Comparing you to that other person because those are the only thought options of relativity.

If you're going to *inspire* people one day, *you can't start from admiration.* ***There has to be steps.***

What I landed on is: as much of a star as I know I am, it's not up to them to see it, it's up to me. And I need them. We need the mailman, the store clerk, the cranky construction worker. These people have lives, too. And we're all just trying to understand each other and co-exist.

Next time you get offended by a "muggle" remember that you don't have to live out a by-stander life, you get to be interesting. Sometimes, that comes with an interrogation.

It heightens our compassion to consider a weaker mind and not react from our ego. It's tough work. But, you can sustain.

Chapter 6: Sustaining

While you try and grow more self awareness, build the life of your dreams, and avoid low frequency conversations with people who aren't in alignment, you also need energy to *live.* How can someone do this all with out going absolutely insane? ***Meditate.***

Or, as I call it: *shutting the fuck up* for a minute.

You think your cognitive brain is in control? You think anything you do is because of the control you have on this wild ride of life? What else has to happen for you to realize there's more to this day than your physical reality?

Try this experiment: Sit in silence (or with frequencies/ binaural beats on).

Close your eyes. Visualize an item. Something you like. Something you wouldn't normally come into contact with. But enjoy very much. Focus on how this thing makes you feel. Keep the feeling of this thing alive by playing with it in your imagination. Hold it. Reach out with your imaginary hands and grab it. Enjoy it. Like a kid on their birthday who just got a gift. Just be there. Don't brag about it. Don't show it off. Just enjoy it. Special for you.

Return here as a happy place, daily, for 7 days. Trying to focus on it for 17 minutes everyday. Even if it's a couple minutes scattered through-out your day at different times, just make sure to come back to it. Don't tell anybody about it.

Do this for 7 days.

Watch this thing show up in your experience. Over and over again. If you create the right amount of head and heart coherency about this thing. You couldn't stop it from attracting to you...

(I did this with white vans for a film I produced. Everywhere. I saw them EVERYWHERE.)

Now, once you prove this theory right. Realize all the negative thoughts you dwell on. Then, observe the feeling state caused by how they make you react.

Remember how that thing showed up in physical form? Imagine all the energetic ways your worries show up when you sit with them continuously. Now, knowing this, do you still choose negative feeling thoughts? *You're a creator. Act like it.*

Sidebar: I do have a theory that some vessels are here to experience the contrast. *You can never insert yourself into someone else's experience to change them.*

Statistically, there ARE unstable people. You can't save the world. Save yourself. And, if someone is interested, they'll knock.

Sustaining the inspiration can be a tricky game, but once you figure this out, you're able to go above and beyond in whatever direction you feel is your calling.

Sometimes it fades for a pulse, but if you have the intention to keep growing and exploring, you won't be measuring your progress so forensically through out the process and eventually, will stop breaking your own heart.

I am a fan of tucking your head and doing the work, but that does sound counter intuitive to being "mindful".

I'd say ***find the balance*** between making progress on that fulfilling reason you began your journey in the first place with holding back until you really ***do feel it***.

Once in a while, *technique moves the spirit,* but ultimately, we're trying to get where the spirit is moving us. When flow state takes over and we achieve everything as we're flying! Letting life reward us, as we float into our desired experiences.

The work of ***allowing***.

Chapter 7: Art of Allowing

So, yo, I knew Daniel Ceasar. *(I said I'd never be someone to say those type of things. But, fuck it, he's great enough.)*

In Toronto, doing shows, I met Daniel before he popped big time. We'd bump into each other at random times. On-stage at friends shows and other trivial ways you'd see fellow musicians in the scene you're both hustling in, to essentially one day, get out of. *He did.* It happened. Right in front of us all.

Later, taking into account how different people I've gotten the pleasure to meet that have taken off, and those that seemingly plateaued.

What was the difference? *How was their energy?*

There's a *grace*. Even if they're *tough*. There's a non- stressed energy about a success. Like, *"it either is, or it isn't"*.

I'd see Daniel get off work at a place on King Street. Working a part time job while he recorded his break out music. As a fellow artist, I remember feeling sorry for him.

Late night job hustling, trynna make it. Little did we know, in a single year, his face would be all over the city on Apple ad's! But, even back then, in his old circumstance, getting off work to bike home at 2:00 am, he still didn't seem worried. *He was okay in the moment.* Grounded and kind. *Incredible.*

Fear and anxiety can consume the best of us at different times. But, there is a deeper knowing that keeps those who really make progress going. Some form of God they tap into before anything makes it to the surface. Some way to quiet the chatter of "what if" and "they say".

I have made it past where I thought I was going to. And only now can I find the confidence to dream higher and own my light. Could you imagine seeing your omega before the proof?

The art of allowing takes the idea that everything great you could possibly dream of, is *already in vibrational form* waiting to come into this dimension to delight and surprise you.

You just have to *let it in.*

The art of it is, the feeling process on how to *allow* it in. Remember that self worth stuff we talked about? *Yes, that.* Be the nose to smell the flower. Be the voice that speaks. Be the wind that blows. Become the expressions of life.

*Find the instrument you are best suited to play and **join the band.** There's more than enough for everyone.*

In a demanding atmosphere like the "3rd dimension", it's hard to not get caught up in connecting on *lack mentality.* The general population loves this activity! It softens the blow that most are not *actually* following their dreams.

As community-driven beings, we love to connect; so we can feel like everyone has a purpose with each other. Where that *can* be true, it's not always the current focus. *Convincing oneself that they are a victim, **takes away the pressure of ever having to change anything.***

When I do private parties as a freestyle rapper, I often find myself in conversation with a guest who's enjoyed yet seemingly *triggered* by what my job is. *I'll explain.*

Sweet as they are, there's another story that surfaces on why they never pursued their own dreams. After I attempted antidotes of guidance for years, I realized...*this was a choice!!* A **truth** they've settled on. Now, part of their identity. They've made a *"story bed"* and they're going to reluctantly lie in it as a participant.

Hyped on a *once-shiny idea.* Time came to create a discipline and they stopped. *Unable to force it.* Wishing they could allow and connect to the root of their practice. In the *Tao.*

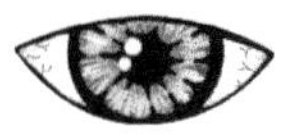

Chapter 8: The Tao

"The *Tao* that can be named is not the *Tao*." - Dr. Wayne Dyer.

Tao de Ching. One of the most profound books ever written. A collection of *poem-like* passages that elude to pure natural law, through the lens of a greater understanding.

The most current English translation by Stephen Mitchell. *The awareness that held the first idea of anything ever.*

The wisdom of the *Tao* has taught me that I'm not in control. The energy of everything that ever was, is still in motion. We are a spec of dust in time and space and get to experience this for a little while. *Make of it what we will.*

Once you accept the powerful inertia of the *Tao*, ***you can only plan to allow.***

The *Tao* has more to do with the "negative space" of the universe than the actual matter that you can see. Not negative in terms of + / -. But, negative space meaning, *not yet manifested.* Open clay in the quantum field. Willing, patient. Always, before time. Everything that is and is not.

Without accepting the ever changing motion of life, you'll always fight against uncertainty. Which kills. ***So, let go.***

It goes deeper the more you consider it. Just know that you're always wanting to be one with it. It serves anything it has created. Constant nurturing loving fibers of the universe. This energy source is crucial to feel. Learn to become one with it by finding your center. It is always available.

More valuable answers come from "the void", then could ever come from a noisy world of calculated guesses.

Become one with the *Tao*. ***Allow*** the inspiration that informs the direction of your fulfillment.

Chapter 9: Flow State

From one who has stood in public and freestyle rapped for hours on end, I can say that flow state is always available. But, not always achieved by the human, *due to ourself.*

"The Zone" flow state happens when one is challenged, yet confident. *Holistically* invested focus. Time bends as you exist in this miracle space. ***You're in spiral of pure infinite energy.***

Engaging in a state of flow is like taping into an unlimited source of ideas, productivity and information. Like your intuition. But, it can literally take over, like you become a larger energetic being. On a vibrational build, like a singing bowl.

I've formatted a process that I guide others with audio chants, breathe-work and awareness practices that offer a glimpse into a pattern based flow state.

Chants, rhythm, movement. Hmm...

Elements familiar to our ancestors tribal behaviour. What were they uncovering with these rituals? *Freedom by virtue of* ***being present.***

Nothing else *exists* when in flow. *Only I can stop me.* Even then, may just need to slow down first, it's a powerful stream. If we can achieve this sort of momentum in *life*. We begin having effortless experiences, creating our *really, really good time.*

Flow state is where I like to get all my work done, if possible. Which, I want to believe it is. It just ties in with *avoiding resistance*. A difficult thing for humans, if we're already focused on the contrast.

What you focus on expands. ***Find a better feeling thought.*** *Harmonize with flow. Immerse yourself in it.* ***It's always available. If you are.***

Chapter 10: Results

Once you see results, you may get addicted to that feeling. It's in our human DNA. Thought + action = reward. We've built thousands of years of evolution around this understanding. Truth is: life isn't always going to give you a celebration cake and a *Rolex* at the end of every finish line. Sometimes, it's just you. Alone.

The team that even made a portion of the trip with you, is gone. Everyone focused on your breakthrough for a moment, so you felt loved and encouraged, but now it's all over. It's up to you to pick up the pieces and continue. Because relying on someone else's energy to push your cart isn't healthy. Find a way to create results *on your own terms.* Key to keeping that harmony going.

Sure! You should recruit teams, adapt and grow by any means! But, never confuse the actual results you're getting. It's you. It's the result of your *feeling state.* Believe it or not, all while you thought it was the physical actions that were turning the wheel, it was the *perception of self* during the act. *So, we **need the action**, but **paired with the feeling** of wellness about the act.*

How you feel causes the manifestation to occur, not just the action. So, the work is never done. When you accomplish what you'd like now, there will be another. And another. So on and so forth. Keeping our emotions in line is the new work.

Enjoy the results at face value. Sometimes you just gotta revel in the good feeling like "I actually did something!" And let that be enough in the present.

Focusing on the *inevitable* next thing, with this light heart of gratitude will *most definitely* create a better one. With out comparing, smile and enjoy what you get.

Chapter 11: Moving Forward, Again.

Look around. The room you're in right now. Do you like it? If the successful version of you walked in this room right now, would they feel happy for the person reading?

If so, congrats! You're on the way to creating an even better life! It's all baby steps from here, if you got your circumstances and setting aligned to your *true form.*

If not, take a minute after you read this chapter to fix a few things up. I don't know what that means to you, but make the choice to un-clutter, wipe down or reorganize. *Do something that will inspire you to cultivate a* ***more focused energy****.*

Start again, but from where you are NOW. You know a lot more today than you did yesterday. You're growing up now. But with the freedom to play like a kid!

Enjoy your space and embrace your life.

I know, it can be tough to dust the dirt off and think you're going to get different results with this same old outfit, personality or energy. And you're right. It is. So, change it. But changes don't happen overnight. That's the part that scares people. The time investment. From an earnest perspective, there's a huge opportunity here. You're going to be alive anyway. Wouldn't you rather have a slow rising stock than no stock? *Fuck it.* Get involved! Toss a *bet on yourself.* Might as well. Because, if you don't make a decision, you're sitting here as a nothing person. And that's a choice.

If you're in a funk, ***go help someone***. It often shows us another side of ourselves when we reach out to offer our services and energy to others. See what value you can offer the world. It feels nice. *And isn't that a great place to start?*

Closing Words from the Author

This book is dedicated to all the dreamers, loners, unsung and real-world healers. You are seen and you matter. Let this work be a reminder to give to yourself as much (or more) than you give to others. Let the temptation of proving yourself or battling for your perceived-worth fade away and your true center come to life.

It's more helpful to everyone if you find peace before you share. Truly love yourself before you try and give that love away. Choose quality over quantity, or else you just got a bunch of shit you don't want.

The exchange for these lessons was pain 90% of the time. So, let these earnings of learnings add to your life's abundance moving forward and maybe even skip a couple steps! Not that you won't have to overcome the exact same or similar or even harder barriers, but you will have a clue card on how to play the game a little better. You'll create space for yourself to find a better feeling thought and move forward with that. After this, you don't have to pretend to not know the answer when you really do. It's always there. It's the thing that scares you the most. The image you're too intimidated to stare towards because you're scared it might be too powerful to come from you. It IS you.

Be well.

Love 'n Light,
Ellevan

More from the Author:

World Record Release
365 Music Videos in 1 year (2018)
youtube.com/ellevanmusic

Disciplined Stoners Podcast (ongoing)
anchor.fm/disciplinedstoners

Films:

- *Sideboob*
- *Nobody Famous*
- *The Ellevan Not For Netflix Netflick Special* (TBD)

The self produced multimedia masterpiece is set to be available for viewing later this year.

If you'd like to get in contact with the author, you can reach out directly by meditating at exactly 11:11 pm EST and set the mental intention to connecting and translating the idea wrapped in love to Ellevan, wherever he may be.

*Alternatively, you can find him on any social platform: @EllevanMusic + He makes music, so search "Ellevan" wherever you stream and enjoy his mindful tunes.

The first draft of this book was written on-set of a movie. The edits happened in between life and music production in the following months. There's never a right time. Do it now.

This book is a product of alchemy.

Credits

STFU: Thoughts and Feelings

Written by Ellevan // www.ellevanmusic.com

Cover artwork and book layout design by
Jade Rakes // www.jaderakes.com

Independently published with KDP

ISBN: 9798530202605

A Life Worth Living

"Beginnings are usually scary,
and endings are usually sad.
But it's everything in between
that makes it all worth living."
- Bob Marley

May you be engaged
in all the right ways, my friend.

www.ingramcontent.com/pod-product-compliance
Ingram Content Group UK Ltd.
Pitfield, Milton Keynes, MK11 3LW, UK
UKHW021934190726
13853UKWH00004B/1429

9 798530 202605